DAILY DEVOTIONS FOR JUNIORS

NO. 2

by
Ruth I. Johnson

moody press
chicago

CONTENTS

3

GOD THE CREATOR

Read the Menu: (Scripture)

"Thou, even thou, art LORD alone; thou hast made heaven, the heaven of heavens, with all their host, the earth, and all things that are therein, the seas, and all that is therein, and thou preservest them all; and the host of heaven worshippeth thee" (Neh. 9:6).

Place Your Order: (Prayer)

Dear Father and Creator, thank you for making everything for your glory. Help me to use it that way—always. Amen.

Eat Your Meal: (Thoughts)

Sometimes people who seem to have many new ideas are called "creative" people. Advertising agencies and radio and television producers are always on the lookout for people who are creative.

But these people are not really creative. God is the only one who has ever "created" anything. People take things that have already been created and bring out new ideas, but God made the world out of nothing.

The Bible tells us that the world had no form; it was empty and dark until God said, "Let there be light: and there was light" (Gen. 1:3). He separated the night from the day, and the sky from the waters. He made the dry land and the heavens.

God even caused the earth to produce food—fruit and vegetables and grain. When God looked over His work, he

4

was pleased with the things He had created. Yes, it was all good.

God made the sun for the day and the stars for the night. He created birds, fish, and animals, both large and small. Finally, God created a man, and gave him a wife. The man, Adam, and his wife, Eve, were placed in a beautiful garden. God told them to take care of everything that He had created.

God told Adam that he could have everything in the entire world except the fruit of a certain tree. But Adam and his wife disobeyed God and took fruit from this tree. This was the beginning of sin in God's world.

Isn't it strange that after Adam and Eve were given everything else in the garden, they should take the one and only thing God said they couldn't have?

But what about you?

God created you. He gave you everything you have. Have you given yourself to Him? Are you willing to live for Him?

Digest Your Meal: (Sum it up)

Since God created me, I should live for Him and live so that others will see what a Christian is.

☑ I have finished today's breakfast with God.

CAIN THE KILLER

Read the Menu: (Scripture)

"If we confess our sins, he is faithful and just to forgive us our sins, and to cleanse us from all unrighteousness" (I John 1:9).

Place Your Order: (Prayer)

Dear Lord, help me to recognize what is sin in my life and to have the courage to confess everything that is wrong. Amen.

Eat Your Meal: (Thoughts)

After Adam and Eve had been sent away from the beautiful Garden of Eden, God gave them two children. The oldest boy's name was Cain; the other one was named Abel. No doubt, Adam and Eve explained to their sons why they had left the garden. They told their boys that when they worshiped God they needed to bring a sacrifice, because of sin. Abel loved God very much, but Cain did not. When it came time to sacrifice, Abel did it because of his love for God. Cain did it because he thought he had to.

When God saw the offerings that were brought by Cain, He could not accept them, because they were not the kind God said He wanted. He knew there was no love in Cain's heart. So, God accepted Abel's offering, but He refused the offering that Cain brought. This made Cain very angry. He was angry not only at God but at his brother Abel. Adam and Eve tried to talk with their son, but Cain would not listen. Instead, he became even more angry.

One day when Cain and Abel were in the field together, they had a quarrel, and Cain became so angry that he killed his brother.

Later the Lord asked Cain, "Where is your brother Abel?" Again Cain became angry. Right then and there Cain should have confessed his sin to God, but instead he became very angry, and said, "I don't know where he is. Do I have to take care of my brother?" Not only had he murdered his own brother but now he was lying about it. But God knew what had happened. He said, "You killed your brother. His blood is there on the ground. As a punishment, you will never find rest on this earth again. You will wander all around and will not have a regular home."

Cain began to think about it, but still he did not confess his sin to God. He was not sorry for his sin, but only afraid that people would hurt him.

God would have forgiven Cain's evil deed if he had confessed his sin. But Cain refused to do this. God can forgive our sin only when we come to God and confess that we are sinners and in need of a Saviour.

Digest Your Meal: (Sum it up)

When you fail to confess even one little sin, you will find it easier to commit another sin, and another, and another. . .

☑ I have finished today's breakfast with God.

NOAH THE NAVIGATOR

Read the Menu: (Scripture)

"Giving thanks always for all things unto God and the Father in the name of our Lord Jesus Christ" (Eph. 5:20).

Place Your Order: (Prayer)

Dear Father, help me to put You first in everything, even in learning to thank You for sparing me from things that could be dangerous. Amen.

Eat Your Meal: (Thoughts)

Noah was born when his father was 182 years old. It wasn't until Noah was 500 years old that God gave him three sons. Their names were Shem, Ham, and Japheth.

There were many people in the world, but most of them were living sinful lives. As God looked down and saw all the wickedness on the earth, He decided to wipe out the entire human race—all that He had created, birds, animals, men, everything. But Noah was an honest and good man. He loved God, and taught his family to love God, too.

One day God told Noah of His plans. "Everything will perish," said God. "But if you will obey and follow my instructions, and build an ark as I tell you to do, you and your family will be spared."

Noah followed God's instructions and built the ark exactly as commanded. When it was finished, God put into the ark a male and a female of every kind of bird and animal that flew in the air or crept on the ground. Noah stored enough

8

food in the ark for both his family and the animals to eat. Then Noah, his wife, Noah's sons and their wives, all entered the ark.

After God closed the door of the ark, the rain began to pour down upon the earth. The rainstorm continued for forty days and nights. The water began to rise higher and higher over the ground. Soon even the mountains were covered, and before long everything that God had created—birds, cattle, wild beasts, and even people—were washed away to their death.

After the flood waters had finally gone down, Noah and his family left the ark, together with all the animals and birds that had been in the ark. Immediately Noah built an altar, and offered sacrifices, and he and his family thanked God for taking care of them and for protecting the birds and animals.

How many times has God protected and taken care of you? How many times have you been spared from trouble, accident, or other harm? How many times have you followed Noah's example and thanked God for all His care and protection?

Digest Your Meal: (Sum it up)

Since I am God's child, He will protect and care for me in ways I do not either see or understand. He spared Noah, and I must trust Him just as Noah did.

☑ I have finished today's breakfast with God.

ABRAHAM THE FATHER

Read the Menu: (Scripture)

"He that loveth father or mother more than me is not worthy of me: and he that loveth son or daughter more than me is not worthy of me" (Matt. 10:37).

Place Your Order: (Prayer)

Dear Lord, help me never to allow anything to become so important to me that I love it more than I love You. Amen.

Eat Your Meal: (Thoughts)

Abraham and Sarah had been married for quite a while, but they did not have any children. God had promised Abraham that he would have a son, but so far no son had been born.

Abraham became impatient, and finally he had a son by Sarah's Egyptian maid, Hagar. This did not please God, for he was not the son that God had promised.

God blessed Sarah and she gave birth to a son when Abraham was 100 years old. They named him Isaac. Abraham loved Isaac, very much, but Abraham loved God even more.

One day God decided to test Abraham's love to see if it was genuine. He asked Abraham to take his only son, Isaac and sacrifice him on an altar. Without question, Abraham obeyed. He took his son and the firewood and together they began the long journey to the place God had told them to go. Abraham placed Isaac on the altar and was about to kill his son as a sacrifice when God called out, "Abraham, Abraham."

Then God spoke to Abraham and said, "Now I know that you do love me."

Abraham was willing to give up his dearest treasure even though he waited 100 years for that treasure to arrive. God sometimes asks us to sacrifice things that are very dear to us. If He should ask you to do this, would you be willing?

What is the dearest treasure you have? Mother? Father? Sister? Brother? Friend? Or "things"? Do these mean more to you than God? Are you making Him play "second fiddle" to something else in your life. If so, that something is sin! Be sure that God has first place in your life.

Digest Your Meal: (Sum it up)

If anything is more important to me than Christ, it is wrong. God wants me to love Him first and to love Him with my whole heart.

☑ I have finished today's breakfast with God.

JACOB THE SCHEMER

Read the Menu: (Scripture)

"Humble yourselves in the sight of the Lord, and he shall lift you up" (James 4:10).

Place Your Order: (Prayer)

Heavenly Father, teach me to be honest before You and everyone else, even when it seems that being dishonest will bring me gain. Amen.

Eat Your Meal: (Thoughts)

Jacob and Esau were twin sons of Isaac and Rebecca. Isaac was an old man and was becoming blind. He could no longer see his sons clearly, but he could tell the differences in their voices. Their skin was different, too. Esau had lots of hair on his arms; Jacob's arms were smooth.

Every Israelite father gave his oldest son a special blessing. Isaac told Esau to get ready for it. When Rebecca heard this, she passed the word on to Jacob. "I will prepare a dinner for your father," she said. "After he eats it, he will give the blessing to you instead of to Esau."

Jacob and his mother schemed together how they would fix the dinner, put some of the animal's skin on Jacob's arms, and in this way fool Isaac.

In a short time Jacob walked into his father's room. "I am Esau," he lied. Isaac was surprised. "Come closer," he said. "I want to feel your arms to see if you are really Esau." Jacob moved nearer to his father. "Your voice is like Jacob's, but your hands are Esau's hands," said Isaac.

"Are you really my son Esau?" Isaac asked again.

Again Jacob lied. "I am."

Isaac took the food, and after he had eaten it, he pronounced a blessing on Jacob.

Sometime later Esau arrived with the food he had fixed for his father. "I am Esau," he said.

Isaac became very sad. Now he knew that he had been tricked into giving the blessing to the wrong son.

When Jacob realized that his twin brother knew what had happened, he ran away from home and went to live with his uncle. From then on Jacob's life was one of scheming and running, scheming and running.

When we try to scheme against God, our lives become filled with fear. If there is sin in your life, be sure to confess it to God, and make things right.

Digest Your Meal: (Sum it up)

Any kind of cheating is sin. Sometimes it seems that very few people think of this as sin anymore. But God says it is wrong, and that it must be confessed and made right.

☐ I have finished today's breakfast with God.

RACHEL THE BELOVED

Read the Menu: (Scripture)

"Teach me to do thy will; for thou art my God: thy spirit is good; lead me into the land of uprightness" (Ps. 143:10).

Place Your Order: (Prayer)

Dear Saviour, help me in all the choices I have to make all through my life. I am not wise enough now, nor will I ever be wise enough to make them without Your help. Amen.

Eat Your Meal: (Thoughts)

Rachel, the daughter of Laban, was sent to the well to get water for her sheep. On the very same day at the very same time, Jacob also came to the well. He talked to Rachel and told her that he was the son of Rebecca. Quickly Rachel ran and told her family. They invited Jacob to come and live with them and to work in their fields.

Jacob's Uncle Laban had two daughters, Rachel and her older sister Leah. After Jacob had worked for his uncle for a month, his uncle asked him what his wages should be. Jacob said he would work for Laban for seven years if he could have Rachel for his wife. Laban agreed.

For the next seven years Jacob worked in the fields, but they seemed like only a few days because of his love for Rachel. Finally, Jacob reminded Laban that the time had come for the wedding. After the wedding ceremony Jacob found that he had been tricked. Leah was given to him as his bride; not Rachel, whom he loved. Now Jacob saw that

14

others could scheme as well as he. After talking it over with Laban, Jacob agreed to work another seven years. This time he was given Rachel, and they were married.

God saw that Rachel was loved more than Leah, so He let Leah have children, while Rachel had none. After a long time, God let Rachel have a son, too, and she named him Joseph.

Rachel had been chosen because she was lovely. She was a beautiful girl and had a "pretty face." The Bible tells us that man "looketh on the outward appearance, but God looketh on the heart." Looks do not always show what is inside the heart.

Whenever we have a choice to make, whether it is a big or small decision, we should talk it over with God to know what is best in the matter. Do you have some wants and wishes? Ask God to show you what is best for your life.

Digest Your Meal: (Sum it up)

Sometimes I make wrong choices because I only look on the surface of things. This is why I need to ask God what is best.

☐ I have finished today's breakfast with God.

JOSEPH THE FAVORITE

Read the Menu: (Scripture)

"And we know that all things work together for good to them that love God, to them who are the called according to his purpose" (Rom. 8:28).

Place Your Order: (Prayer)

Heavenly Father, do things with my life to "make me, mold me, fill me and use me," all for your glory. Amen.

Eat Your Meal: (Thoughts)

Because Joseph was the first son born to Jacob's favorite wife, Rachel, he also became a favorite to his father, Jacob. The sons of Leah noticed this. One day Jacob gave a special, colorful coat to Joseph. This made the other boys hate Joseph all the more.

While Jacob's older sons were out taking care of the sheep one day, Jacob became worried about them. He asked Joseph to go and see if everything was all right. While Joseph was still some distance from the place where his brothers were working, they saw him coming. Suddenly they decided to kill him.

"We can say a wild beast has devoured him," said one of the boys. Reuben, the oldest in the family, thought it would be better just to take away his beautiful coat and throw him into a pit rather than kill him. The other boys finally agreed with Reuben.

After Joseph had been thrown in the pit, a caravan of

Ishmaelites came by. The brothers talked it over and decided it would be a good idea to sell Joseph to the Ishmaelites, who would then take him to Egypt. Then they took Joseph's coat and dipped it in the blood of a goat.

That night when the brothers returned to their home, they brought Joseph's coat to their father. "We found this coat," they said. Jacob was very sad, for it looked as though Joseph had been killed by a wild animal. Jacob mourned for his son for many days.

But God had a plan. There were some lessons that both Joseph and his brothers needed to learn, and God used this way to teach them these lessons.

Sometimes when things come into our lives that do not look very good, we should stop and remember that God may be trying to work out something in our lives to make us more like Him.

Do you have problems? Troubles? Tests or trials? Accept them cheerfully, knowing that God can use these very things to work out something very special in your life. He did it for Joseph; He can do it for you.

Digest Your Meal: (Sum it up)

Sometimes God uses members of my family to teach me and them some lessons that we need to know. I must learn to accept everything that comes from Him.

☐ I have finished today's breakfast with God.

17

BENJAMIN THE SUBSTITUTE

Read the Menu: (Scripture)

"For I reckon that the sufferings of this present time are not worthy to be compared with the glory which shall be revealed in us" (Rom. 8:18).

Place Your Order: (Prayer)

O Lord, I am as precious to you as Benjamin was to Jacob. Let me remember this even when I feel alone and forgotten by everyone else. Amen.

Eat Your Meal: (Thoughts)

After the disappearance of Joseph, Jacob showered all of his attention on Rachel's other son, Benjamin.

When food began to be very scarce in the land of Israel, Jacob told his sons to go to Egypt, for there was food there. When they arrived in Egypt, they talked to the assistant to the great Pharaoh. What Jacob's sons did not know was that this man was their brother Joseph.

They did not recognize him as their brother. But Joseph recognized his brothers immediately.

Earlier in his life Joseph had had a dream about all the members of his family bowing down before him. Now the dream had come true. There, kneeling before him, were the sons of Jacob, begging for food. When Joseph saw his youngest brother, Benjamin, he was deeply moved. Quickly Joseph left the room because he did not want to cry in front of his brothers.

While his brothers were eating, Joseph gave orders to his servants to fill each sack with food. He also told them to place his silver cup in Benjamin's sack. The next morning, shortly after Jacob's sons began their journey home, one of Joseph's servants caught up with Joseph's brothers and accused them of stealing his master's silver cup. The servant examined the sacks and found Joseph's silver cup in Benjamin's sack. Joseph's brothers were frightened. Judah said that they had not stolen the cup. He tried to explain that unless Benjamin could be released to go home with them, their father would surely die. Then he told how Benjamin's older brother, Joseph, had died, and now if Benjamin the dearly beloved child of Jacob's old age were to be put into prison, it would be more than the old man could bear.

All the brothers traveled back to Joseph's house with his servant, and when Joseph heard the pleadings of the brothers to spare Benjamin for the sake of their father, Joseph wept aloud and told his brothers who he was.

God had used Joseph's misfortune to save Jacob's entire family from starvation. Arrangements were made for Jacob and all his people to move to the land of Egypt. There they were well cared for all through the famine.

Digest Your Meal: (Sum it up)

God used Benjamin to soften Joseph's heart, to frighten Judah and his brothers, and to unite Jacob's family. Maybe God has a special work for me, too. I will be listening for His voice to call me.

☐ I have finished today's breakfast with God.

MOSES THE LEADER

Read the Menu: (Scripture)

"But my God shall supply all your need according to his riches in glory by Christ Jesus" (Phil. 4:19).

Place Your Order: (Prayer)

Let me learn to trust You, Lord Jesus, with both the big and small things in my life. Amen.

Eat Your Meal: (Thoughts)

When Moses was born, because the Egyptians had made a law which said that all Jewish baby boys were to be killed, his mother put him in a little basket and placed it among the reeds near the riverbank. While Moses was in the basket, Pharaoh's daughter found him and adopted him as her son.

One day after Moses had grown up, he saw one of the men of Israel being mistreated by an Egyptian. Moses became angry and killed the Egyptian. Then he ran for his life. Moses spent the next forty years in the desert feeding and caring for sheep.

It was while Moses was tending sheep in the desert that God appeared to Moses and let him know that he had seen how cruelly the people of Israel were being treated. God told Moses that He had chosen him to lead the people of Israel out of Egypt and away from the wicked Pharaoh. Moses told God that the people of Israel would not believe that God had spoken to him. Then God performed a miracle by changing Moses' shepherd's staff into a snake, and by changing it back into a staff. God told Moses that if he performed this miracle before the children of Israel, they would believe that God had appeared to him.

Moses believed God would be with him and was not afraid to take the message of God to Pharaoh. The Lord sent several plagues upon the land of Egypt: frogs, boils, hail, locust, darkness, and finally the oldest child in each Egyptian family died. When Pharaoh saw that he could not fight against God any longer, he said to Moses, "Go and serve the Lord."

The Israelites began their journey and soon came to a wilderness. Here, there was no food. But God provided bread from heaven called manna. All the way to the promised land, God provided clothing, food, rest, and shelter for the people through their faithful leader, Moses.

God always takes care of those who completely trust in Him. He has promised to supply "all" our needs.

Digest Your Meal: (Sum it up)

The Baby Moses could not be kept in his own home because of the king's edict to kill all the boy babies in the homes of the Israelites. But God provided Moses with another home when Pharaoh's daughter adopted him as her son. While he was in her home he received the education and training he needed to become leader of the people of Israel. Moses found God faithful in providing every need of the people of Israel when he led them out of Egypt into the wilderness on their way to Canaan. God provided them with food and water and kept their clothes and shoes from wearing out. If I am God's child, He will provide for my every need just as He provided for the needs of Moses and his people.

☐ I have finished today's breakfast with God.

21

CALEB THE COURAGEOUS

Read the Menu: (Scripture)

"And the LORD, he it is that doth go before thee; he will be with thee, he will not fail thee, neither forsake thee: fear not, neither be dismayed" (Deut. 31:8).

Place Your Order: (Prayer)

Dear Father, give me the courage to do what is right, whether anyone else does it or not. Amen.

Eat Your Meal: (Thoughts)

After the people of Israel had lived in the desert for two years, Moses told them that they were to go forward and take over the land that was before them. The people wanted to conquer the land, but first they wanted someone to go in and look over the country. God told Moses to choose one man from each of the twelve tribes and send them as "spies" to look over the land of Canaan. When the men were ready to leave, Moses gave them their final instructions, telling them to look over the country, the people, the city, their armies, and their food.

After forty days, the twelve men returned. They brought back pomegranates, figs, and bunches of grapes so big that two men had to carry them between them on a pole.

"This land is flowing with milk and honey," they said to Moses and the people. "These grapes show how good the food is. But," continued the spies, "we can never go into the land and conquer it, because the cities are too big. They have heavy walls around them and the people are like giants."

As Moses listened to the reports he realized that only ten of the men gave this kind of report. Two others were still waiting for their turn to speak.

"It is true," said Caleb finally. "The people are tall and much stronger than we are." By this time the people of Israel were murmuring. "But we can gain the victory," finished Caleb.

The people seemed to forget that God was leading them. When they thought about the giants and the big cities, they felt as small as grasshoppers.

Moses and Aaron felt very sad when the people decided not to go. Joshua and Caleb were very sorry, too. They begged the people to obey God and believe Him, but the people would not listen. Instead they began to throw stones at Joshua and Caleb. They refused to go into the land that God had promised to give them.

Digest Your Meal: (Sum it up)

Even though a thing may seem impossible to me, if I know it is God's will, I must go ahead. Nothing, or no one, can stop me, for when God is on my side, nothing can really be a "giant" to me.

☐ I have finished today's breakfast with God.

JOSHUA THE REPLACEMENT

Read the Menu: (Scripture)

"I will instruct thee and teach thee in the way which thou shalt go: I will guide thee with mine eye" (Ps. 32:8).

Place Your Order: (Prayer)

Lord, help me to see that nothing is ever impossible when you are with me, but let me really believe that absolutely everything is possible. Amen.

Eat Your Meal: (Thoughts)

Moses had died, and God needed another man to be the leader of the people of Israel. He needed a man who would trust him, who would obey His commands, and who would do as he was told, even if the instructions did not always seem especially practical.

Joshua had been one of Moses' spies. He had come back with a report that the people of Israel could conquer Jericho, even though most of the other spies seemed to feel they could not do it. Because of his complete trust and confidence in God, Joshua was chosen to fill the vacancy left by Moses' death.

Time after time the people of Israel found themselves facing serious problems and war. When they arrived at the city of Jericho, they found that it was closed in by great walls. God told Joshua not to let this frighten him but to follow instructions very carefully. "March around the city once every day for six days," said God. "On the seventh day, go around

24

seven times. When the priests blow their horns, let all the people shout, and the walls of the city will fall down."

For six days the people marched around the city once each day. On the seventh day, they started very early in the morning and marched around Jericho seven times, just as God had told them to do. The seventh time around, the priests blew their horns and the people began to shout. Immediately the walls fell down, and the people were able to take over the city. Joshua and his people had obeyed God's instructions, even though they did not understand them. God blessed and rewarded them because of it.

Do you know what God's will is for your life? If you do know His will, perhaps you do not understand it. But to be really happy, you must obey it. God will bless all who follow His instructions without hesitating or asking, "Why?"

Digest Your Meal: (Sum it up)

God is always looking for faithful "replacements" for His work. With His help, I want to prepare myself spiritually so that if He needs me, I will be ready.

☐ I have finished today's breakfast with God.

DELILAH THE DECEIVER

Read the Menu: (Scripture)

"Submit yourselves therefore to God. Resist the devil, and he will flee from you" (James 4:7).

Place Your Order: (Prayer)

Help me Lord, as I choose my friends, to choose the kind that will help me rather than draw me away from You. Amen.

Eat Your Meal: (Thoughts)

While Delilah pretended to be a friend to Samson, she was really a spy for the Philistines, who were enemies of the country of Israel.

Samson, one of Israel's men, had outstanding strength. He had godly parents and a good home. Samson thought his girl friend, Delilah, loved him dearly, but Delilah had him fooled. Samson was "blinded" by Delilah's attention. She was his girl and that was all that seemed to matter.

Delilah had been promised thousands of dollars by her country if she would find out the true source of Samson's strength. So she set out to get the information.

The first time she asked him why he was so strong, Samson told her he would lose his strength if he were tied up with seven fresh wood fiber cords that had never been dried. Delilah tried this, but soon found that he had lied. The next time he told her that new rope had to be used. When she tried this, she found that he still had not told her the truth. At the third request, Samson told her to weave his hair, but after Delilah followed these instructions, she found that he had not told her the true story.

Now, she made up her mind to get the real truth about what made Samson so strong. She began to nag Samson and beg him for the truth. When he told her he would lose his strength if his long hair would be shaved from his head, she realized that this time he was giving her the true story.

Quickly Delilah went to the Philistines and passed on the information. Later, while Samson was sleeping, Delilah called for a man to shave off Samson's hair. His strength went from him, and the Philistines found it easy to capture him.

Satan had been successful in getting Samson to choose the wrong kind of friend, for Delilah was an enemy spy. This once strong man of Israel became weak, and his enemies gouged out his eyes, and put him in prison.

Digest Your Meal: (Sum it up)

Do I have "friends" who are leading me to sin? Do they suggest, tease, nag, and finally succeed in getting me to do things that are not pleasing to God? If so, I need to change friends.

☐ I have finished today's breakfast with God.

27

RUTH THE FOLLOWER

Read the Menu: (Scripture)

"Thou wilt shew me the path of life: in thy presence is fulness of joy; at thy right hand there are pleasures for evermore" (Ps. 16:11).

Place Your Order: (Prayer)

Father in heaven, help me to become so unselfish that You will always be first in my life. I want others to be second and myself last. Amen.

Eat Your Meal: (Thoughts)

Ruth loved Naomi, her mother-in-law. But now that Naomi had decided to leave Moab to return to her own land, Ruth was very sad. Both women were widows. Naomi's husband had died many years before, and Ruth's husband died after they had been married only ten years.

"Stay here with your people," said Naomi to her daughter-in-law. "And may the Lord treat you as kindly as you have treated me."

"I am going with you," replied Ruth.

Naomi shook her head. "No, go back. Why should you go with me?" she asked.

Ruth looked at her mother-in-law and said, "Don't urge me to desert you by turning away from you. Wherever you go, I will go. Wherever you live, I will live. Your people will become my people. Your God is my God. Where you die I want to die."

Naomi argued no more when she saw that her daughter-in-law was determined to go with her.

When the two women arrived in the city of Bethlehem, Naomi's hometown, Ruth took a job working in the grain fields. There she gathered the grain that the harvesters dropped. She worked from early morning until late at night.

Boaz, the owner of the land where Ruth gathered, had heard how kind she had been to her mother-in-law, and because of this he asked the men to drop some extra grain for her.

After some time Ruth and Boaz were married. God blessed their marriage and gave them a son whom they named Obed. The Bible tells us that Obed was the father of Jesse. Jesse's son was David, and through his descendants came the Lord Jesus Christ, the Saviour of the world.

Ruth made the right choice when she told Naomi that she wanted to live where Naomi lived, to serve where Naomi served, and to worship and love the God Naomi worshiped.

Digest Your Meal: (Sum it up)

Is God on the top of my list? Is He first in my life? Or do I let my own wishes and desires come first? Because Ruth chose that which was best, God blessed her life, and through her family came Jesus, the Saviour of the world.

☐ I have finished today's breakfast with God.

BALAAM THE UNWILLING PROPHET

Read the Menu: (Scripture)

"Have not I commanded thee? Be strong and of a good courage; be not afraid, neither be thou dismayed: for the Lord thy God is with thee whithersoever thou goest" (Joshua 1:9).

Place Your Order: (Prayer)

Dear Saviour, help me always to listen for your voice as you tell me which way to go. Help me to know when to speak and when to be quiet and listen.

Eat Your Meal: (Thoughts)

Balaam was a prophet of God. The king of Moab knew about him, so he sent some men to Balaam's home to ask him to come and curse the people of Israel. When Balaam did not come, the king sent other men to go and visit him—many more of them this time. They were told to give Balaam anything he wanted, just so long as he would curse Israel.

Balaam talked with God about it. God told the prophet that he could go with these men, but he must say only what God told him to say, nothing else.

As Balaam got on his donkey and began his journey, he started to think about the wonderful offer the king of Moab had made. All at once, Balaam's donkey stopped. Then, turning, she ran out into the open field. Balaam beat the donkey until she got back on the regular path. The donkey stopped a second time, and a third time. The third time the donkey stopped, Balaam became very angry and he hit the donkey harder than before.

Then, much to the surprise of Balaam, the donkey opened her mouth and began to speak. "Why did you beat me three times?" she asked.

Balaam told the donkey that she had not served him well, but the donkey insisted that she had carried him around faithfully for many years and never before had she refused to go anywhere Balaam wanted her to go.

Suddenly the angel of the Lord appeared before Balaam. This same angel had stopped in the pathway earlier, and that was why the donkey could not go ahead. The angel reminded Balaam again that he must be very careful to speak only the things that God told him to speak—no more.

Even though the king of Moab wanted Balaam to curse the people of Israel, and offered him money and great honor, Balaam could not curse Israel, for God had told him to bless them.

Digest Your Meal: (Sum it up)

I must learn to listen carefully, for God has many different ways of talking to his children and warning them of danger.

☐ I have finished today's breakfast with God.

SAMUEL THE LISTENER

Read the Menu: (Scripture)

"Bow down thine ear, and hear the words of the wise, and apply thine heart unto my knowledge" (Prov. 22:17).

Place Your Order: (Prayer)

Teach me, dear Lord, how to read Your Word quietly so that I will know when You are trying to talk to me. Amen.

Eat Your Meal: (Thoughts)

Samuel's mother, Hannah, had prayed very earnestly for a son, and God had promised to give her a boy. Hannah not only prayed, but she also made a promise. "If You will give me a son," she had said, "I will give him to the Lord all the days of his life." When Samuel was born, Hannah did just this. When he was a little older, she took him to the temple and presented him to Eli, the priest. "This is the boy I prayed for," she said. "The Lord has given me what I prayed for and, therefore, I hand him back to God for as long as he lives."

One night while Samuel was sleeping, he was awakened when he heard a voice. He thought it was the voice of Eli, so he got up and ran to Eli and said, "Here I am, for you called me."

Eli said, "I did not call you; go and lie down."

Again Samuel heard the voice, and again he ran to Eli. "Here I am, for you certainly called me."

But Eli said, "No, I did not call you. Lie down again." When Samuel heard the voice for the third time, Eli said,

"Go, lie down once more, and when you hear the voice, say, 'Speak, Lord, for thy servant is listening.'"

God did call again, and the boy said, "Speak, for thy servant is listening."

In the morning after Samuel had gotten up and had opened the doors of the temple, Eli said to Samuel, "What message did God give you?" Samuel told him everything.

Samuel had been listening carefully to God's voice and knew exactly what God wanted. Do you live so quietly that you can hear God calling you? Or is your life so filled with activity and action, noise and excitement, that there is never a time for God to speak quietly to you? God's Word says, "Be still, and know that I am God."

Listen for God's voice. Read His Word. Pray to Him, asking for His will to be made clear for your life. Then, like Samuel, say, "Speak, Lord, for I am listening."

Digest Your Meal: (Sum it up)

Even though most of my day is filled with activity, I must learn to set aside some times of quietness so God can talk to me and I can talk to Him.

☐ I have finished today's breakfast with God.

DAVID THE SHEPHERD

Read the Menu: (Scripture)

"I will go in the strength of the Lord God: I will make mention of thy righteousness, even of thine only" (Ps. 71: 16).

Place Your Order: (Prayer)

Oh, Lord in heaven, help me to realize that you can use even me if I as a Christian am living a life that is filled with Your love. Amen.

Eat Your Meal: (Thoughts)

David was home caring for his father's sheep while David's brothers were away at war against the Philistines. With the Philistine army was a nine-foot giant named Goliath. He was dressed in a bronze helmet, a coat of armor, and bronze leggings, and he carried a huge spear. As he came before the army of Israel, he shouted, "Choose a man to represent you and let him come to fight with me. If he is able to kill me, then we shall be your slaves. But if I kill him, then you will be our slaves and serve us." As Saul and the other members of the army of Israel heard the challenge, they became frightened.

One day David's father asked him to take some bread to his brothers at their army camp. As he arrived, he heard the challenge of the giant and offered to go in and fight this enemy. David's offer was reported to King Saul who commanded David to be brought to him. Saul looked at young

David and said, "You will not be able to tackle this Philistine; you are still young, and he is a warrior."

David explained to Saul how he had killed a lion and a bear while taking care of his father's sheep, and he said, "The Lord, who rescued me from the claws of the lion and bear, will rescue me from the hand of this Philistine."

Saul then offered to let David use his armor and weapons. But David said, "I cannot go with these, for I have not proved them." If he was going to face the Philistine giant, he would do so in the name of the Lord. This he did.

David went to meet the giant with his slingshot and five smooth stones which he picked up from the brook. On his first throw he hit the Philistine giant in the forehead, and he dropped to the ground. Then David killed the giant with his own sword. God helped David to conquer because David trusted in Him.

Everything we do must be done in the name and in the power of the Lord. When we do things in our own strength, we will always fail. But when we do things in the strength of the Lord, so that his name receives glory, we will be victorious.

Digest Your Meal: (Sum it up)

If God could use a young shepherd boy to deliver an entire nation, then He can surely use me some place in His service.

☐ I have finished today's breakfast with God.

JONATHAN THE FAITHFUL FRIEND

Read the Menu: (Scripture)

"A man that hath friends must show himself friendly: and there is a friend that sticketh closer than a brother" (Prov. 18:24).

Place Your Order: (Prayer)

Help me today, dear Lord, to be friendly to someone who needs to know that You love them very much. Amen.

Eat Your Meal: (Thoughts)

Jonathan was the son of King Saul, but he was not to be the future king. God had commanded Samuel to anoint Jesse's son, David, to be king after Saul's death. Since Saul was jealous of David, the young man's life was in danger.

Jonathan and David were very close friends, so Jonathan warned David that the king planned to kill him. Jonathan even went in and talked to his father on David's behalf. This helped, and David was once again called into Saul's presence to play his harp for the king. But Saul became angry again. One day he threw his spear at David, but David dodged the spear and escaped.

Later Jonathan again demonstrated to David his true friendship. "I will find out how my father really feels," said Jonathan. "If he is at peace with you, I will let you know, so that you can come back. If he still wants to kill you, I will give you a sign." When Jonathan talked to King Saul, he found that he was still furious and was just as fully determined to kill David as before.

As had been prearranged, Jonathan signaled by the way he shot some arrows that it was unsafe for David to return. As the two friends met at a secret place later, Jonathan said, "Since we have sworn to each other in the Lord's name, the Lord be the mediator between you and me, also between my descendants and yours forever." David and Jonathan separated then. Jonathan returned to the palace, and David went away.

Jonathan proved himself a true friend, even at the expense of his own convenience, comforts, and his own position in life.

In order to have friends, we must show that we are friendly. We read this in God's Word. A true friend is unselfish. He thinks of the other person before he thinks of himself.

Digest Your Meal: (Sum it up)

Friends are helpful, and I want to be a true friend to someone, just as Jesus is a true friend to me.

☐ I have finished today's breakfast with God.

ELIJAH THE FEARLESS

Read the Menu: (Scripture)

"But without faith it is impossible to please him: for he that cometh to God must believe that he is, and that he is a rewarder of them that diligently seek him" (Heb. 11:6).

Place Your Order: (Prayer)

Dear Father, help me to conquer fear, for when I put my faith in You, I don't need to be afraid of anyone or anything. Amen.

Eat Your Meal: (Thoughts)

Ahab was the king of Samaria. His wife, Jezebel, was a very wicked queen. Ahab was not a strong-willed man, so he did almost anything his wife suggested. She was a worshiper of Baal and decided that all the prophets of God should be killed. Most of the prophets were frightened, but Elijah decided to make a visit to the palace. Standing before King Ahab he said, "There will be no more rain in the land until I say so."

There was already a famine in the land, so the lack of rain would be disastrous. When Jezebel heard what Elijah said, she became even more angry than before, and determined to have Elijah killed.

But God sent the prophet to live out in the open by a brook called Cherith. Here he had water to drink, and the ravens came in the morning and in the evening to bring him food.

After the famine had been going on for three years, Elijah

made a proposition to King Ahab. He said, "You call the 450 prophets of Baal together on Mount Carmel, and let us decide once and for all if the Lord is God or if Baal is God."

All the prophets of Baal came to the assigned place. They brought a bullock, cut it up, and laid it on the open altar filled with wood. Then they called for Baal to set fire to it. All the prophets of Baal called to their god from morning until evening, but with no results.

Finally, it was Elijah's turn. He built an altar with twelve stones. He placed the wood in order, and cut the bullock in pieces and laid it on the wood. Then he asked the people to pour water over the altar. They did. Then he told them, "Do it again." Again they poured water over the sacrifice. "Do it a third time." When water filled the trench that Elijah had dug around the altar, he called upon his God to send down fire. Then the fire of God came down and burned up the bullock, and the wood, and the stones, and the dust, and even the water that was in the trench. When the people saw it, they shouted, "The Lord He is God."

Elijah had dared to trust His God. He had been fearless because his faith was in the one and only true God.

Digest Your Meal: (Sum it up)

My faith is in the same God that Elijah trusted. It is not the amount of my faith that counts, but rather God's faithfulness. I must trust Him for something special today.

☐ I have finished today's breakfast with God.

JEZEBEL THE WICKED

Read the Menu: (Scripture)

"Grudge not one against another" (James 5:9).

Place Your Order: (Prayer)

Thank You, Lord, for taking care of everything—even for punishing those who do wrong. Amen.

Eat Your Meal: (Thoughts)

Ahab was a weak-willed king with no backbone, but his wife, Jezebel, was just the opposite. She showed her power in many fierce and different ways.

One day Ahab was pouting. He had thrown himself on the bed facing the wall; he even refused to eat. When Jezebel entered the room and saw her husband, she said, "Why do you behave like this?"

King Ahab explained, "I want that vineyard that belongs to Naboth, and I have made him all kinds of offers, but he won't sell it to me."

Jezebel looked at her husband. "What kind of.a king are you?" she said. "Don't you have authority to get anything you want? Never mind, I'll get Naboth's vineyard for you."

So Jezebel planned a party. She invited Naboth and many others to attend. At the party she got several people to agree that they had heard Naboth curse both God and the king. According to the law, anyone who did this would have to be put to death. So Naboth was put to death.

Queen Jezebel's scheme had worked! Now she went into

Ahab's room, and said, "Rise, and take over the vineyard. Naboth is dead." So the spoiled, weak-willed king went to take possession of Naboth's vineyard.

But God does not allow wickedness to go unpunished. Just as the king went to claim the land, there at the end of the vineyard, stood Elijah. He said, "Your wife has murdered Naboth to get this vineyard. The Lord's punishment is about to come upon you. Also, Jezebel, your wife, will be devoured by dogs."

And everything came to pass just as Elijah said it would happen.

We do not ever need to try to "get even" with anyone who wrongs us. Let God take care of them.

Digest Your Meal: (Sum it up)

I must be careful not to hold a grudge against anyone, nor should I wish evil on those who have been mean to me. I must leave all judgment to God.

☐ I have finished today's breakfast with God.

ELISHA, SUCCESSOR TO ELIJAH

Read the Menu: (Scripture)

"Delight thyself also in the Lord; and he shall give thee the desires of thine heart" (Ps. 37:4).

Place Your Order: (Prayer)

Heavenly Father, make me to see how careful I need to be in making requests of You. Amen.

Eat Your Meal: (Thoughts)

Elisha knew that God was about to call the Prophet Elijah into heaven. "I must go to Bethel," Elijah said to Elisha one day. "You stay here."

But Elisha said, "I will not leave you." So they went together to Bethel.

Again, God sent Elijah to Jericho, and once again Elisha said, "I will not leave you." So they went together to Jericho.

A third time Elijah said, "Stay here, for the Lord has sent me to Jordan."

But Elisha replied again, "I will not leave you." So the two men went together to the Jordan River.

When they came to the river, Elijah took his coat, folded it and struck the water. When the river parted, both men were able to go across on dry ground. When they came to the other side, Elijah said to the younger man, "Ask anything you want before I am taken away."

Elisha wisely replied, "Let a double share of your spirit be upon me."

"You have made it a very difficult request," said Elijah, "but if you see me taken away from you, your request will be granted. If you do not see it happen, you will not get your request."

As the two men walked along, a chariot of fire and horses of fire suddenly came between them, and Elijah was taken up to heaven in a whirlwind.

When young Elisha saw it, he cried, "My father, my father, the chariot of Israel and the horsemen thereof!" Then Elisha took the prophet's coat that fell from Elijah, folded it, and struck the waters of Jordan with it, saying, "Where is the Lord God of Elijah?" The waters of Jordan parted before him, and he crossed over. When the other prophets who were watching saw what had happened, they knew that Elijah's spirit had come upon Elisha, just as he had asked.

When Elisha asked for a double portion of Elijah's spirit, he did not do it selfishly. He made this request because he felt he needed God's power to be able to follow in Elijah's footsteps and serve God and glorify Him.

Digest Your Meal: (Sum it up)

When my motive is right, I can ask anything I want, and God will give it to me. For then it will bring more glory to His name.

☐ I have finished today's breakfast with God.

ESTHER, A BRAVE QUEEN

Read the Menu: (Scripture)

"Ye have not chosen me, but I have chosen you, and ordained you, that ye should go and bring forth fruit, and that your fruit should remain: that whatsoever ye shall ask of the Father in my name, he may give it you" (John 15:16).

Place Your Order: (Prayer)

Dear Heavenly Father, thank You for choosing me to be Your child and Your helper. Amen.

Eat Your Meal: (Thoughts)

King Ahasuerus was a man who expected, when he commanded something to be done, that his orders would be carried out. One day his wife disobeyed him, and he was so displeased that he took away her position as queen and began to look for another woman to replace her. Esther, a very beautiful Jewess, was chosen to be the new queen.

One of the king's princes was a man named Haman. Whenever Haman came through the king's entrance, all other people were asked to bow in respect to him. However, Esther's cousin, Mordecai, refused to bow to Haman. This made Haman very angry. He became so angry that he plotted to kill Mordecai. He wanted all other Jews to be killed too.

Haman had a gallows built which he planned to be used for hanging Mordecai. When Mordecai realized what Haman was doing, he went immediately to Queen Esther and asked her to go before the king and plead for the lives of all the

44

Jewish people. Esther promised to do so, even though she knew it could mean her own death.

Esther was not only a beautiful woman but a wise woman. When she talked to the king she did not make her request right away. Instead, she invited the king and Haman to a banquet. It was during this banquet that she told the king what Haman was planning to do to her people the Israelites. When the king heard this, he became angry, and announced that Haman, rather than Mordecai, would hang on the gallows.

Queen Esther was used to save the lives of the people of Israel because she was not afraid to do what she knew was right.

Digest Your Meal: (Sum it up)

Though Esther was a queen, she risked her life to plead with the king in order to spare the Jewish people from being destroyed. I, like Esther, must always use the courage God gives me to stand up for what is right, even if I am alone.

☐ I have finished today's breakfast with God.

JOB THE TESTED

Read the Menu: (Scripture)

"For ye have need of patience, that, after ye have done the will of God, ye might receive the promise" (Heb. 10:36).

Place Your Order: (Prayer)

Dear Lord, help me to remember that Jesus always intercedes for me even though Satan tries to accuse me. Amen.

Eat Your Meal: (Thoughts)

Job was a very wealthy man, and he had a nice family— seven sons and three daughters. But neither Job's money nor his family took his thoughts away from God.

One day Satan talked with God. He told Him that Job feared God only because he had been given so many possessions. In order to prove to Satan that this was not true, God gave the devil permission to take away some of Job's possessions. One after another, things were taken. His house, his animals, his servants, and even his family were taken. But in all of this, Job did not sin, nor did he ever accuse God of treating him wrong.

God said to Satan, "Have you ever seen a man like Job?"

Satan replied, "He would not be so good if he had some suffering in his own body."

God gave Satan permission to test Job with illness. Soon Job's body was filled with boils. Job's wife became very discouraged. She told Job to curse God. But, the Bible tells us, "In all this Job did not sin."

During his sickness Job's three friends came to visit him. Instead of helping or encouraging him, they told Job that he was suffering because he had sinned. Job knew that he had not sinned against God, and his faith stayed firm and true. To his friends, Job said, "Though he slay me, yet will I trust in him: but I will maintain mine own ways before him."

Job had been a wealthy man, but now he had lost his wealth, his home, his family and his health. God was pleased when He saw how Job stayed true to Him through all his suffering and trials. And God did something wonderful for Job. He gave him twice as many sheep, camels, asses, and oxen as he had owned before, and He gave him seven more sons and three daughters. God never forgets faithfulnessess. He always rewards.

Digest Your Meal: (Sum it up)

Satan accuses *me* before God, too. Do I give him reason to do so? If so, God is not being honored in my life and He cannot bless me as He blessed Job.

☐ I have finished today's breakfast with God.

JONAH THE RUNAWAY

Read the Menu: (Scripture)

"Being confident of this very thing, that he which hath begun a good work in you will perform it until the day of Jesus Christ" (Phil. 1:6).

Place Your Order: (Prayer)

Dear Lord, help me to be listening to hear Your voice, and to be willing to go wherever You lead when You call me for Your service. Amen.

Eat Your Meal: (Thoughts)

God called Jonah to be a prophet of the Lord. One day the Lord asked Jonah to go to Nineveh and warn the people that their city would be destroyed unless they repented of their sins. But Jonah was not a very good prophet. He decided that he would not obey God. Instead of going to Nineveh, he went to Joppa, a city on the seacoast. When he arrived in Joppa, he found that a ship was loading and almost ready to sail for Tarshish. Jonah bought a ticket and got on the ship, hoping to run away from God.

Jonah was very tired, so he went to the bottom of the ship and went to sleep. As the big ship began to leave the shores, the sky turned black. A storm was coming up! The winds began to howl and the waves mounted higher and higher, and soon the ship was rolling from one side to another. The sailors aboard ship were terrified, and wondered how Jonah could sleep through the storm. They awoke him, and said,

"Get up! Pray to your God that we will not be destroyed!" Jonah knew what was wrong. He was running away from God, and now God was sending this storm to punish him.

"What have you done to make your God angry?" asked one of the sailors.

"God called me to go to Nineveh to preach," explained Jonah. "But instead of obeying God, I tried to run away from God. I know how the sea will become calm, so follow my instructions. If you will throw me in the sea, the storm will cease."

At first the sailors refused, but when Jonah insisted that this was the only way to calm the storm, they threw him overboard. In a moment the raging water became calm. The sailors realized God had quieted the sea. As a result, they offered a sacrifice to the true and living God, and made promises to Him.

Jonah did not drown because God had prepared a great fish to swallow Jonah. After he was three days and three nights in the belly of the fish, Jonah prayed to his God, and the fish vomited Jonah upon the dry land. Then Jonah obeyed God's call to preach against sin in the city of Nineveh.

Digest Your Meal: (Sum it up)

If God calls me to work for Him, I want to obey. God has ways of making His children listen to His voice and do the things that are right.

☐ I have finished today's breakfast with God.

DANIEL THE TRUE-HEARTED

Read the Menu: (Scripture)

"I can do all things through Christ which strengtheneth me" (Phil. 4:13).

Place Your Order: (Prayer)

Father, help me to be brave when I'm tempted to be afraid.

Eat Your Meal: (Thoughts)

Even though Daniel was young when Nebuchadnezzar captured the people of Judah and brought them to Babylon, he too was taken prisoner with some other boys. All of them were sent to a special school since they were to become helpers of the king. They were given some of the king's special food, because everyone wanted them to have strong bodies.

Daniel and three of his friends—Shadrach, Meshach and Abednego—were in the same school. From the very beginning, these four boys decided that they would be true to God no matter what happened.

Daniel and his friends had been brought up to observe the law of God given to the people of Israel through Moses. According to this law, the people were forbidden to eat certain meats. For this reason Daniel and his friends felt they could not eat the menu planned for the young men in the palace school. Even though it took a great deal of courage, Daniel went to the chief of the house and said, "Let us be on our own diet for ten days. We will eat vegetables and drink water. We will not take the king's wine. After ten days you can

50

check to see if we are weaker or stronger." The chief of the house agreed.

For ten days Daniel, Shadrach, Meshach, and Abednego ate bread and vegetables. Instead of drinking wine, they drank water. Later, when Melzar, the king's overseer, examined them, he found that they were much healthier than any of the other young men.

Sometime later King Nebuchadnezzar had a meeting with all of the young men who had gone through the course of training for service in the palace. He too saw that Shadrach, Meshach, Abednego, and Daniel were ten times better than all the other men in the country of Babylon in all matters of wisdom and understanding. The king liked these boys very much and decided to train them for a very important work.

God allowed Daniel and his friends to become captives so He could use them in the king's house. We can be thankful they had the courage to stand up for what was right.

Digest Your Meal: (Sum it up)

I need and can have the same kind of courage Daniel and his friends had. They stood up for what they believed, and the king respected them for it.

☐ I have finished today's breakfast with God.

RAHAB THE PROTECTOR

Read the Menu: (Scripture)

"But love ye your enemies, and do good, and lend, hoping for nothing again; and your reward shall be great, and ye shall be the children of the Highest: for he is kind unto the unthankful and to the evil" (Luke 6:35).

Place Your Order: (Prayer)

Dear Lord, help me to see people who are in need, and then may I show them that You are the only one who can really help them. Amen.

Eat Your Meal: (Thoughts)

After Moses had died and the people had mourned the loss of their leader, it was time for Joshua to take over the leadership. He called the officers together and told them to instruct the people to get ready to march. While they were preparing for this, Joshua sent two spies to visit the city of Jericho. When the spies came to the wall of Jericho, they saw a house. A woman by the name of Rahab lived there.

While Rahab was not an Israelite, she did believe that God had given this land to the people of Israel. Because she believed the God of Israel was the true God, she hid these two men so the soldiers of Jericho could not find and kill them.

These men from Israel were very thankful and promised her that neither she nor any member of her family would be harmed when the armies of Israel came to conquer the city. They told her to hang a red rope on the outside of the window so that all of the people of Israel would see which house to leave unharmed.

Before the spies left, Rahab told them to go to the mountains to hide for three days before they returned to their camp. Then she let them down the wall by a rope.

When the spies finally returned to their camp, they not only told Joshua about the enemy but they also told him how Rahab had protected them.

Later when Joshua led his people into Jericho every one was destroyed except Rahab and the members of her family. Because Rahab had faith in God and showed kindness to some of God's people, God rewarded her by protecting both her and her family.

We should never do a kindness in order to get a reward, but we must remember that God does reward those who show kindness to His children.

Digest Your Meal: (Sum it up)

If I show kindness to those who seem to be my enemies, they may see that they need Christ as their Saviour too.

☐ I have finished today's breakfast with God.

NATHAN THE OUTSPOKEN

Read the Menu: (Scripture)

"Create in me a clean heart, O God; and renew a right spirit within me" (Ps. 51:10).

Place Your Order: (Prayer)

Heavenly Father, help me to see that I can never hide anything from You, because You even know the secrets in my heart. Amen.

Eat Your Meal: (Thoughts)

David's wife, Bathsheba, gave birth to a fine baby boy. King David loved his son, but somehow he was not really happy. David knew he had sinned, but he had not confessed his sin nor had he asked God to forgive him.

One day when Nathan the prophet came to visit the king, he told David a story. He said, "Once upon a time there were two men—one rich and one poor. The rich man had many sheep and cattle, but the poor man had only one little lamb. One day when the rich man had some visitors, he went out and butchered the poor man's lamb and served it to the people. The rich man had many sheep of his own, but he saved them and took the only lamb the poor man had."

When David heard this story he became very angry. "That rich man should be killed," said David. "He has done wrong."

The prophet turned to King David and said, "You are that man."

David may have thought that his sin would not be found

54

out, but the prophet knew that Bathsheba had been the wife of Uriah, and David had sinned to get her. He had even put Uriah in the front of the battle so that he would most certainly be killed. And he was killed.

Suddenly David realized how terribly he had sinned. Right there, in the prophet's presence, he bowed his head and said, "I have sinned against the Lord."

God forgave David for this terrible sin, just as He will forgive us when we come and confess that we have sinned. David cried to the Lord and said, "Create in me a clean heart, O God." He was really sorry for his sin, and God forgave him. But even though God forgave David, God had to let the nation of Israel and the enemies of God know that God is a holy God—that He cannot overlook sin. So Nathan told David, "The Lord has put away your sin. You shall not die. But because by your sin you have given great occasion to the enemies of the Lord to blaspheme, the child that has been born to you and Bath-sheba shall surely die." Later God blessed David and Bathsheba by giving them another baby, whom they named Solomon.

God cannot let sin go unpunished, but when we confess our sin, God will bless us again.

Digest Your Meal: (Sum it up)

I should be careful how I live, and when I see that I have done wrong, I must confess it right away. Then God can bless me again.

☐ I have finished today's breakfast with God.

55

ABSALOM THE PROUD

Read the Menu: (Scripture)

"But he giveth more grace. Wherefore he saith, God resisteth the proud, but giveth grace unto the humble" (James 4:6).

Place Your Order: (Prayer)

Dear Lord, I know You love to lead Your children. Let me learn to walk slowly, quietly, and patiently in order that I will always follow you and never get ahead of You. Amen.

Eat Your Meal: (Thoughts)

David's son Absalom saw that some of the people did not like David as king. So Absalom decided that he would be the right man to be king. He began to make plans for it. Absalom was a very nice-looking prince; he was tall and had especially beautiful hair.

Before long, many of the people began to turn to Absalom. He had appointed men to go all over the country to speak for him, and soon the people began to shout, "Absalom reigns." This is just what the young prince wanted.

One day while David was away from Jerusalem on business, Absalom decided it was time for him to take over the throne. The people became very confused. Should they be loyal to King David, or should they accept Absalom as their new leader? Since there were two sides, it wasn't long before there was fighting. When David returned and heard it, he too became confused. He wanted his men to be victorious, but at the same time he did not want anything to happen to his son Absalom.

On the first day of battle 20,000 men on Absalom's side were killed. Somehow Absalom became separated from his army. While he was all alone, the mule on which he rode became frightened and started to race toward a big oak tree. As Absalom went under the low branches, his long, beautiful hair caught on the branches and there he hung as his mule ran on. One of David's soldiers saw him hanging there and killed the young prince. Then he sent word to King David that his son was dead.

God had not planned for Absalom to become the king. But Absalom didn't care about that. He wanted to do things in his own way. And he found that his way led finally to defeat and death.

God's way is always the best way. We must learn to wait cheerfully and patiently for the Lord to work out His will for us.

Digest Your Meal: (Sum it up)

When I take things into my own hands before asking God to show me His will, there is only one direction that I can go—down to defeat.

☐ I have finished today's breakfast with God.

57

NAAMAN THE LEPER

Read the Menu: (Scripture)

"Whatsoever he saith unto you, do it" (John 2:5*b*).

Place Your Order: (Prayer)

Heavenly Father, I want to follow where You lead and not question You on anything. Help me to do this. Amen.

Eat Your Meal: (Thoughts)

Naaman was a great general. He was head of the Syrian army and a very important man. On one of his army's raids on Israel, they had captured a young girl who now was a slave and worked in the general's home.

Even though the great general held a high position and had won many victories, he had one great sadness in his life. He had a sickness called leprosy. No doubt he had gone to many doctors, but not one was able to help him. As the leprosy became worse, he realized that soon he could no longer live with his people. He would have to go to a leper colony.

The little Jewish slave girl heard about the general's sickness. She knew that he had gone to many people for help. She also knew his illness had not improved. One day she went to the general's wife and told her that she knew someone who could cure the general from his leprosy. The little girl said she was sure that Elisha the prophet was in Samaria and would be able to help General Naaman. Naaman's wife told him right away. Immediately Naaman went to the king and asked and received permission to take the trip to Samaria.

As General Naaman faced the prophet Elisha, he was told to go to the Jordan River and wash seven times. This made the great general very angry. Why should he, an important general, go and wash in a dirty, old river? Rather than do this, Naaman decided to go home. On his way home, his servants who were with him said, "If the prophet had asked you to do some great thing, you would have done it. So why not do this?"

Naaman listened to his men, and finally agreed to go down to the Jordan River. There he dipped himself one, two, three —yes, seven times, just as Elisha had said. As he came up from the water the seventh time, he saw that all of his leprosy had disappeared.

Simple obedience was what God required of Naaman. We, too, must be obedient and do whatever God asks us to do.

Digest Your Meal: (Sum it up)

God often uses simple methods to show people His power. I must be careful to follow every instruction given in His Word.

☐ I have finished today's breakfast with God.

NEHEMIAH THE BUILDER

Read the Menu: (Scripture)

"So built we the wall; and all the wall was joined together unto the half thereof: for the people had a mind to work" (Neh. 4:6).

Place Your Order: (Prayer)

Dear Lord, I want to be as ready as Nehemiah was to do whatever work needs to be done for Your people. Amen.

Eat Your Meal: (Thoughts)

Nehemiah was a godly man. While he was a servant for the king of Persia, he got the news that his own people were having a very hard time in Jerusalem. Nehemiah knew that things would be much better if only the city wall could be rebuilt to keep the enemies out.

Nehemiah was so sad about the situation that he actually sat down and cried. But he knew that tears would not help build the wall, so he began to pray to God. And then the thought came to him that maybe he could be the leader. Perhaps Persia's King Artaxerxes would give him permission to return to Jerusalem and help his people. As he prayed, he asked God to open the heart of King Artaxerxes.

One day Artaxerxes asked Nehemiah why he was so sad. This was his opportunity to tell the king that he wanted to return to Jerusalem to help rebuild the walls. After explaining to King Artaxerxes his wish, the king gave him permission to leave. More than that, the king wrote letters to the

60

governors of the places Nehemiah would pass through on his way to Jerusalem. He asked each one to help Nehemiah all they could. Then he sent some of his own captains and horsemen to go with Nehemiah.

After Nehemiah arrived in Jerusalem, he rested for three days. One night, while everyone else was asleep, Nehemiah went out and looked at the walls that had been destroyed. They were in ruins. Rubbish was lying all over the ground. Nehemiah felt that the walls must be rebuilt immediately. He enlisted the interest and help of the people, and soon everyone was working. The enemy tried to stop the building of the wall. But they were unsuccessful, for Nehemiah's faith was in God. The people, too, were trusting Him to enable them to do the job of rebuilding the wall.

For the next 52 days the Jewish people worked from early morning until late at night repairing the wall. Finally, it was finished, and Jerusalem again became a strong and safe city. It was their refuge from the enemy.

Digest Your Meal: (Sum it up)

God is always my refuge and strength. He is a very present help. I must learn to trust Him for everything. He is my Leader.

☐ I have finished today's breakfast with God.

61

ISAIAH THE FORECASTER

Read the Menu: (Scripture)

"If we live in the Spirit, let us also walk in the Spirit" (Gal. 5:25).

Place Your Order: (Prayer)

O, Lord, help me to be able to accept both good and bad news, and help me to learn something from both easy and hard experiences. Amen.

Eat Your Meal: (Thoughts)

Because Isaiah was a prophet, he was able to give information to the people that the Lord first gave to him. One of the things that Isaiah prophesied was the birth of the Lord Jesus. God promised Him as the Redeemer for the people of Israel and the entire world.

Hezekiah was king of Judah during Isaiah's time. During Hezekiah's reign, the king of Assyria threatened to come and conquer Judah. Hezekiah told his people not to be afraid. Why? Because the king of Assyria only had men to fight for him, but the people of Israel had God on their side.

But later Hezekiah too became afraid. He went to the temple to pray, and then sent for Isaiah the prophet. Isaiah received a message from the Lord which again told Hezekiah and his people not to be afraid of the wicked king of Assyria, for God would bring great punishment upon him.

When the king of Assyria sent a threatening letter to Hezekiah, he went to the temple and spread it before the Lord.

He prayed earnestly that God would spare him and Jerusalem, and not let the wicked king of Assyria take over.

God heard Hezekiah's prayer and told Isaiah the prophet that He would protect the city, also that the enemy would return to his own land without coming into the city or even shooting an arrow into it. Everything that Isaiah prophesied, came true. That night 185,000 Assyrians were killed by one of God's angels. When the king of Assyria saw this, he went back to his own land, and there was killed by his own sons.

Shortly after this, Hezekiah became sick. Isaiah came to him, this time to bring bad news. He said, "Make all things ready, for you are going to die." This made Hezekiah very sad. He prayed and wept, asking God to spare his life. The Lord heard his prayer, and sent Isaiah to tell him that he would be well in three days, and would have fifteen more years to live.

Through the years of his life, Hezekiah became a very wealthy king. Even though Hezekiah and his nation had received many blessings from God, he did not remember to give God credit. Hezekiah's heart was lifted up with pride, but later he repented, so God didn't allow the king of Babylon to come and take the people of Israel captive until after Hezekiah died. Then, as Isaiah had prophesied, the riches God had given Israel were taken away to Babylon. Hezekiah's sons also were taken to Babylon—as captives.

God's forecaster, the Prophet Isaiah, had to bring both good and bad news to King Hezekiah.

Digest Your Meal: (Sum it up)

May I live so that God can give His very best to me.

☐ I have finished today's breakfast with God.

THE SUMMARY

In this book you read about the one and only Creator, God. You also learned about many people who lived long ago.

You read of Cain, who hated and killed his brother Abel. You met Jacob, who learned that others could scheme, too. You read about jealousy when Joseph was his father's favorite.

Then there was Moses, who felt unable to lead his people, but who found God faithful. You learned of Caleb, a courageous spy, who disagreed with the majority. You met Joshua, Moses' replacement. You saw the strongest man, Samson, become weak when deceived by a beautiful woman. You heard a talking donkey shock a prophet. You met Samuel, who listened to God; and David, who bravely killed the giant Goliath. You observed two loyal friends, David and Jonathan. You met Elisha, successor to the great Prophet Elijah. You read how a beautiful queen, Esther, risked her life to save her people's lives.

You read about a runaway prophet, Jonah, and a brave teen-ager in a foreign land, Daniel. Next came Nathan, who was not afraid to speak out against sin—even to his king. You saw a proud and foolish son, Absalom, bring grief to his father David. You met Nehemiah, who had the vision for rebuilding the walls of Jerusalem, and got permission to do that very thing.

Have you put yourself in the place of any of these people? Can God bless you, as He did some of these, or must He let hard things come into your life to bring you back to His way? Think about these people, and learn from their experiences. God will always give you strength to do what is right.